C000075679

THE
Archive Photographs
SERIES

LONGDENDALE
AND
GLOSSOPDALE

This dandy, photographed at about the turn of the century, in Hollingworth, is included in this book to represent all the many individuals who appear on surviving old photographs and about which we now know little or nothing.

THE
Archive Photographs
SERIES

LONGDENDALE
AND
GLOSSOPDALE

Compiled by
Bill Johnson

CHALFORD

First published 1996
Copyright © Bill Johnson, 1996

The Chalford Publishing Company
St Mary's Mill, Chalford,
Stroud, Gloucestershire, GL6 8NX

ISBN 0 7524 0659 0

Typesetting and origination by
The Chalford Publishing Company
Printed in Great Britain by
Redwood Books, Trowbridge

Dedication
To my wife, Barbara

Contents

Th'Owd Village Green

None very far from we'ur aw live,
Ther's a little bit o' greawnd,
That's bin a good deal luckier,
Than t' rest o't land areawnd.
Fer it hasno' so far been enclosed,
Bi somedy made o' brass,
Nor had notice booards put up to say
Yo mun 'Please keep off the grass!'

Un i' summer time, when t' neets are fine,
Un t' larks sing up it sky,
O't little lads com troopin' up,
From t' village, just close by.
They usen it fer a cricket greawnd;
Aw've had monny a heawr's fun
When aw've stood theer un watch't 'um,
Just before ther gams begun.

Its a gradely treat to see 'um,
When they'n getten onto't greawnd;
Poo off ther caps un jackets,
Un then go struttin' reawnd,
Pretendin' to examine t' crease,
To see it ther's it way
Onny bits o' pot or stones, or owt
That'll interfere wi't play.

Un then ther captain foot fer sides
Or else say pick or bang,
Un monny a time ther language
Is a good de'ul woss than slang;
For some on 'um swears most awfull,
If their mon does' no win,
Un they an't go a fielden' eawt,
While tother lot goes in.

Ber soon they settle'n deawn to t' game,
Un then ther is sich cheers,
If one brings off a champion catch,
Enough to crack yer ears.
Ber if he fails to tek it,
Which happens monny a time,
Well – aw darno quote verbatim,
In fact, it wouldno' rhyme.

Yo'll yer one sheawt 'Stond further back,
Hoo's towd thi' t' stond so near';
Another 'ul say, 'Com moor this road,
He allis plays 'um here.'
Un thus they keepun fratchin',
Till they'n getten' o't side eawt,
Un then they fair mek t' welkin' ring,
Wi ther merry joyous sheawt.

Un when they'n o' had inins reawnd,
Un darkness gathers o'er,
They rushen off to th'owd barn dur,
To see hoo'us get yed score.
Un when they'n put ther jackets on,
Gone whoam their different ways,
Ther's monny a time aw stop behiend,
Un think o' my young days.

Ther's monny a time when aw think o't lads
That's played on't same owd green;
Aw wonder we'ur they'n getten to,
Un whether ther still't bi seen.
Ther's some aw know are deud un' gone,
May they never from memory fade,
Nor ever com a time aw'st cease
To think with whom aw played.

Tummylow

Acknowledgements

The author is indebted to Mrs D. Fitton for typing the text
and to the people listed below who generously allowed him to use their photographs:
Mr F. Bamford, Mr and Mrs Berry, Mr J. Chatterton, Miss P. Cowley, Mr H. Peel,
Mr F.A. Powell, Mr F. Robinson, Mr E. Sidebottom, Mrs D. Sowerbutts, Mr C. Wood.

Introduction

The past has been described by L.P. Hartley as a foreign country. Indeed when we glimpse the past from photographs we are struck by the strangeness of images that are set within a familiar landscape. It is this mixture of the familiar and the foreign that provides our past with so much that is interesting and important to us. We need to know where we came from in order to understand who we are. In Longdendale and Glossopdale we are fortunate that, in an era when change has been rushed through at a speed unthinkable to our forebears, so much of what seems a slower and more stable past remains for us to explore.

The very outline of the landscape of the two Dales still bears all the marks of the ice and water that created them. The vast ice sheet that covered northern Britain some 10,000 years ago smoothed and flattened out hill tops to produce the accordant summits of the moorlands tops that dominate our skyline. The power released when the ice melted and the water tore down the hillside caused the slumping and sliding of shale and sandstone that marks the valley sides to this day. The melt water that was borne away carved the mighty valley of the Etherow, which when joined by the Goyt forms one of the major river systems of northern Britain – the Mersey Basin. Thus two vital gifts were bequeathed by these momentous events that were to dominate the subsequent history of the two Dales. These were the access through the high Pennines provided by these deep valleys that had been carved into the Millstone grit and the plentiful water that flowed within them.

The strategic significance of the valley for the movement of both goods and armies across the grain of the country were quickly appreciated. Celtic peoples built their hill fort on Mouselow in the Iron Age to be replaced by the Roman fort of Melandra – both designed to control the important Pennine crossing. Later in the Middle Ages another conqueror, this time William I, brooked no opposition to his punishment of the north. In the winter of 1069 his mercenary army destroyed every village in the Etherow valley, such that, even twenty years later, Domesday Book could not find a single person or beast to record in the valley. With the return of more peaceful times strategic interests were served by either the direct royal ownership of land or by the granting land to powerful nobleman such as the Dukes of Norfolk or the Earls of Stamford, who could be relied upon to protect upon to protect royal interests. The woods clothing the valley sides were soon cleared by the tenant farmers to allow the development of livestock and some arable farming. Overlooking this activity through the centuries from the Middle Ages stood Mottram church – its distinctive profile offering guidance and welcome for the men and their pack mules loaded with Cheshire salt or Yorkshire wool that negotiated the inhospitable wilderness of Bleaklow. As manufacturing activity expanded in the growing towns of the Lancashire plain and the West Riding of Yorkshire, the rudimentary mule tracks and remnants of Roman roads proved inadequate requiring the construction of Turnpikes and other metalled roads. The first of these was cut in 1732, another in 1765 and finally a new road was built from Hyde to Mottram in 1832. Mottram and Old Glossop served the needs of the increasing numbers of thirsty travellers, leaving us a legacy of packhorse and coaching inns. Mule pace, however, was too slow for the nineteenth-century age of industrialisation and the cotton town of Manchester required fast connection by rail to the steel town of Sheffield. Accordingly, hundreds of navvies were brought here to dig the two Woodhead tunnels which were opened in 1845 and 1852. The appalling conditions suffered by these men is witnessed in their graves and memorials found at the Woodhead chapel. The age of steam has left us with an often sadly neglected and under-employed heritage of fine railway architecture, comprising spectacular, ornate station buildings and bridges.

Water provided the other element that fashioned the area. Fast flowing and clear Pennine streams and rivers not only watered the pasture lands, but were also adopted as the force to drive the wheels of industry. Grain milling and woollen fulling mills were the first to employ this abundant supply of energy, resulting in the development of a widespread domestic woollen industry by the eighteenth century. Weaving lofts and sheds from this period can still be traced in many villages. It was, however, the arrival of cotton, which when coupled with steam power, completely transformed the rural dales into vital industrial communities. Quiet villages that numbered their populations in hundreds in the late 1780s measured them in thousands by the 1850s. Complexes of cotton mills, with their imposing chimney stacks began to line the river banks as landowners realised the profits that could be made by leasing or selling land and water courses to enterprising mill owners. In the case of the Howards this was achieved on the grand scale by the design and construction of a complete industrial new town that has become Glossop.

The capping rocks of durable gritstone exposed by those long ago glacial meltwaters were extensively quarried to house the vastly expanding workforce. The industrial slums of a 'Cottonopolis' were not for this area. The workers' housing was of durable gritstone, simple but airy and solid in construction. Gritstone is honey coloured, soft and malleable when first worked by the stonemasons but quickly develops a hard shell when exposed to air. Unfortunately in doing so the outer layers of the stone absorbed and were stained by the sulphurous smoke of thousands of coal fires and mill chimneys. The resultant blackened exteriors gave the valley communities a characteristic if somewhat forbidding appearance.

Water was to play another major role in the evolution of out landscape. The thirst of the burgeoning city of Manchester found a response in the construction of the worlds first major urban water supply. The Longdendale reservoir stands as a monument to one of Victorian England's most outstanding engineers, John LaTrobe Bateman. Today we are the happy recipients of his wonderful use of stonework. If only our current road engineers were half as perceptive as this man was!

Despite the decline of the cotton industry in the late nineteenth and early twentieth century, the sense of community that had been established persisted in religious and sporting activities. In the present century the two dales have been increasingly riven by a multitude of administrative boundaries that has led to increasing confusion in terms of planning and development. Recovery in recent years has been the expansion of the communities, such that they snuggle together even more tightly in their niches within the valley. More enlightened methods of stone cleaning and clean air acts have arrested the decline in the building stock, which once again shows a honey coloured and renovated face. It is perhaps ironic that the facility of communication, so influential in the development of the area, now threatens its future as the congestion and pollution of motor traffic choke the narrow streets of the valley communities.

John Hamshere
August 1996

One
Rural

Throstle's Nest, Tintwistle.

Hodge Fold, Broadbottom in the 1930s. The barn on the right has been demolished.

Hodge Fold, Broadbottom. The mill on the skyline is now used by 'Progressive Woodworking'.

Bottoms Hall Wood, Broadbottom in the 1890s.

Moss Lane, Broadbottom.

Deep Cutting, Mottram, seen from Hough Hill, Stalybridge.

Mudd Farm, Mottram. The farm has now been replaced by a large dwelling and outbuildings.

Old Hall Lane, Mottram. The grounds of the hall are on the right.

A later view of the lane following removal of the gates.

The Isolation Hospital that once stood in Carr House Lane, Mottram.

Nine Arches Bridge, Woodhead. The Angel Inn, on the right in this picture, has long gone.

Shearing time at Snake Pass in 1930. In 1807 the Shepherds' Society listed five members in Woodhead, one at Enterclough, one at Hey, one at Croddin Brook, two at Highstones, two at Hollens, three at Arnfield, two at Hollingworth Bank and one at North Britain.

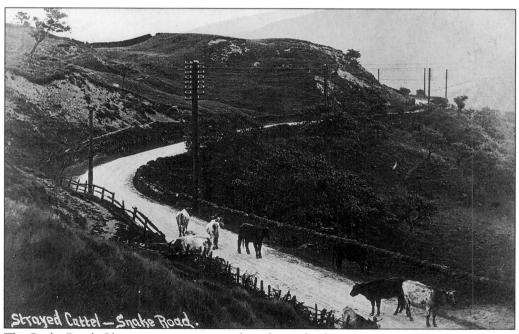

The Snake Road, Glossop in quieter times than those of today.

A snowdrift in Arnfield Lane during the memorable winter of 1947.

Snow near Crowden in 1947 being cleared by Cheshire County Council workmen.

A North Western bus battling through the snow in Longdendale in 1947.

Arnfield Bridge in the 1930s.

Arnfield in the 1930s. The landowners were the Manchester Corporation Waterworks who kept the walls in good repair and installed robust ladder stiles and gates.

Gamekeepers of Longdendale counting their catch.

Higher Bank Farm, Tintwistle was farmed by James Hague.

Lower Bank Farm, Tintwistle was farmed by Raymond Hartle. There was a third farm in this area, called Middle Bank Farm, but all are now gone.

Bent Terrace, Meadow Bank, Hollingworth.

Thorncliffe Cottages were known as the 'Dog Kennel'.

Thorncliffe Hall Farm, Hollingworth, was farmed by the Bradleys.

Bent Meadow seen from the 'Dog Kennel'.

The entrance to Thorncliffe Hall, Hollingworth.

Cow Lane, Hollingworth in the 1940s.

Two
Houses and Buildings

Water Lane, Hollingworth.

Mottram Moor in the 1930s.

Looking north up Stalybridge Road, Mottram. The buildings on the hillside were chalets built between the wars on Hobson Moor Road and Dewsnap Lane, used either as weekend or permanent homes. Four of them still remain.

Deep Cutting, Mottram with the Roe Cross Inn on the right in 1911. The road was opened in 1826 to provide a better gradient for the stage coaches going down to Mottram. It took twelve years to complete and a large quantity of stone was removed.

Deep Cutting, Mottram with Lower Roe Cross Farm on the left in Edge Lane. In 1904 the Stalybridge, Hyde, Mossley and Dukinfield Joint Board started an electric tram service from Stalybridge finishing at the Dog and Partridge at the Stalybridge boundary on the other side of the Cutting. Passengers bound for Mottram then had to walk to continue their journey.

Cottages at Spout Green, Mottram.

Surviving buildings of Hyde Brook Farm, Mottram, prior to demolition for development of industrial units on the old tannery site.

Market Street, Mottram in the 1920s.

Church Brow, Mottram in earlier times. The cottages beyond the steps and the Black Bull Inn behind have since been demolished.

Mottram church vicarage on what is now Ashworth Lane. A row of council houses now fringes the field site. Broadbottom Road is beyond.

Hyde Road, Mottram. The Co-op is on the left with Mottram House on the right.

Harewood House, Broadbottom, now in ruins and awaiting the development of this whole site.

Market Street, Broadbottom in the early 1900s. Harewood House grounds are on the right and 'Mottram' railway station, as it was called for many years, is on the left.

Market Street, Broadbottom. Harewood House is beyond the row of cottages.

Old Glossop Cross.

A view from Dinting Arches looking towards Glossop.

Chew Wood Mill, Chisworth. Built in 1795 by the Rowbottom family it manufactured cotton banding for mill machinery. It also contained a dye works and produced khaki cloth during the Boer War. The mill, and some cottages, are to the left of the photograph and the accommodation for the workers is on the right.

The George and Dragon at Woodhead, now demolished.

This is Woodhead and the building on the right is the old Rose and Crown, now gone.

Millbrook, Hollingworth before 1938 when the road was widened at this point.

Woolley Mill Farm, Hollingworth.

Etherow Cottages, Hollingworth were converted by Bill Sowerbutts into Etherow Lodge. There is a stable block on the left.

Walker's Engraving Works, Bent Mill, Hollingworth.

Market Street, Hollingworth.

Market Street, Hollingworth.

Market Street, Hollingworth.

Salt Box Houses, Tea Row, Hollingworth in the early 1880s.

36

Manor Cottages, Market Street, Hollingworth.

Arnfield Tower, Tintwistle in 1904 was built in 1850 for J.F. Bateman the engineer for the Longdendale Reservoirs. In 1977 it was converted for use as a field study centre for Manchester school children but fell victim to Manchester Council's cost cutting and closed in 1995.

New Road, Tintwistle. Bridge Mill wall is on the left.

The Fountain, Tintwistle, erected in 1902
to commemorate the coronation of
Edward VII.

The junction of Old Road and Church Street, Tintwistle. The fountain can be seen again here, in front of the Liberal Club.

The fountain has suffered a modern conversion and now forms the base of an electric lamp standard introduced in 1938. Note the RAC motorcycle and sidecar. This photograph was taken in the days when RAC and AA patrolmen saluted member motorists on the road.

Woodhead Road, Tintwistle.

Slurring Stones, Old Road, Tintwistle.

40

The Cenotaph in Tintwistle. The cannon on the right came from the Crimean War and the proprietor of the Bull Inn in the background around this time was Mr Rowbottom.

The Manse, Manchester Road, Tintwistle.

Ogden House, Arnfield Moor is now just a name on the map on the way to the shooting cabin.

Bleak House, Crowden. The high circular chimney pots were, no doubt, designed to combat the strong valley winds.

Crowden Hall was built in 1692 and was the home of the Hadfield family. John Hadfield was born here in 1803. He was married three times, jailed twice and eventually executed for forgery. The life of this rogue is featured by Melvyn Bragg in his book, *The Maid of Buttermere*. The Hall was demolished in 1937.

'The Hut', Crowden.

Crowden Village 1927, 'The Commercial' in the foreground was demolished at the turn of the century. The long row of cottages in the background are now used as a Youth Hostel which was opened in 1965.

Chew Wood Mill, Chisworth. A close view of the mill and the cottages. The building developed from the right hand side, the join with the new addition can be seen close to the central door. The cottage on the left was built in 1842 to house the Rowbottoms whose family initials are on the date stone in the wall. The mill lodge is in the front. The mill closed in the late 1930s and was pulled down in the early 1960s. The end cottages remain, as does the hole for the lodge and the houses shown earlier in the photograph on page 31.

Three
Trade

Lee Vale rope works, Charlesworth.

Two electric trains, known as 'Bo Bos', pulling trucks of sand through Broadbottom Station during British Rail's programme of sand blasting.

Lower Market Street, Broadbottom. At the end of the road can be seen the 'Foresters' where there is now a garden created by the local Amenity Society some years ago.

The inaugural bus service between Broadbottom, Mottram and Hollingworth on 1 July 1905. The single fare to Hollingworth was three pence. This group is posed on Broadbottom Road, Mottram where modern bungalows now front the road.

The Red Bull's Head, Mottram. In the picture are, left to right: the daughter of Mr Greenhalgh, George Mettrick, Chris Hinchcliffe, Greenhalgh junior and his father.

Spout Green Mill, Mottram. This once steam-driven mill was built in the 1880s.

Spout Green, Mottram. A rear view of the mill and old cottages which once housed hatters and handloom weavers.

The Admiral Tollemache, Lane Ends, Mottram in 1927. This building is now a dwelling.

The Savoy Cinema, Mottram opened in 1927 and closed in 1956. Houses now occupy this site at the junction of Mottram Moor and Back Moor.

Botany Print Works from Best Hill, Charlesworth.

Best Hill Mill, Charlesworth, 1914/18. The mill was used for the manufacture of shells during the war. Munition workers in the picture are, left to right: Clemence Smith, Joe Hilton, Mrs Bromley, young Cockayne, -?-, Annie Longson, Olive Bowden, Clarence White, Agnes Hadfield.

An Olive and Partington Tiger Tractor taking a delivery of wood along Victoria Street to the paper mill at Turnlee.

Waterside Mill, Hadfield undergoing demolition in March 1977.

Woodhead Station. This Gothic looking structure was built, no doubt, to impress the shareholders rather than to blend into the Pennine landscape. The crenellated tunnel opening behind it continues the theme. It was said that in the time of steam trains the expressions on the faces of the gargoyles on the tunnel reflected the reactions of passengers as they coughed and gasped through the three miles of smoke-filled tunnel!

Three Woodhead tunnels have been cut under the Pennines to Dunford Bridge in Yorkshire at different times. The first opened in 1845, the second in 1852 and the third in 1954. The older tunnels closed to rail traffic in 1954 and were used to carry electricity powerlines instead.

Brown's Bleach works, Crowden. The buildings are still there today but in a ruinous condition.

Crowden Station in the 1950s. Electric trains arrived on the Woodhead line in 1954.

The Commercial Inn, Crowden.

The George and Dragon, Woodhead in the 1950s. This inn closed in 1961 and was just one of many to have been lost in the valley over recent years. Others closed include; Quiet Shepherd, Angel, Rose and Crown, Royal Oak, Commercial, Tollemache Arms, Shepherd and Crook and Millers Arms.

The Tollemache Arms in Holme Moss Road was a teetotal inn.

Millers Arms, Saltersbrook.

The Old Paper Mill at Crowden. This was formerly known as Kidfield Mill and is now converted as a dwelling.

A delivery of beer from the Macclesfield Brewery, in the care of John Green of Macclesfield, suffers a mishap near the Beehive Inn, Tintwistle in 1927.

Market Street, Hollingworth in the 1920s. A delivery of petrol is being made to the chemist shop. The petrol pump can be seen on the pavement.

Sevilles, Cannon Street, Hollingworth.

This is Green Lane in Hollingworth. Harrisons the newsagents are on the left and Booths the grocers on the right.

Market Street in Hollingworth. The man standing on the kerb opposite the Organ Inn, with a telephone outside, is Arthur Gomersal.

The Hollingworth Co-op in Market Street in the 1920s. The houses on the immediate right are known as Sophie Row.

This is W. Merrill making a delivery for Walter Booth in Woolley Lane, Hollingworth.

A selection of Walter Booth's transport, Hollingworth in the 1930s.

Walter Booth in Hollingworth.

The blacksmiths shop at the Gun Inn, Hollingworth.

Mr Harrison was very keen that his customers should buy the *Sunday Graphic* at his shop at the corner of Green Lane, Hollingworth! Today his shop, like the *Sunday Graphic*, is no longer available.

Market Street, Hollingworth in the 1920s. To the left of Wain's butchers was Merrill's greengrocers. The shop on the right was Marsden's sweetshop but it has now gone and cars are parked on the space.

Walter Booth's shop on Market Street, Hollingworth. He transported mainly corn in these vehicles.

The River Etherow Bleaching Company, Mersey Mills, Hollingworth.

The yard and offices of the Manchester Corporation Waterworks at Bottoms Reservoir.

Bottoms Reservoir Quarry, Tintwistle in 1895.

The Lee Vale Rope Works, Charlesworth. In the photograph, from left to right, back row, are: F. Wood, M. Cooper, A. Beard, M.A. Stafford, A. Sandiford, Mrs Birtles. Middle row: Mrs Kief, Mrs Phillips, P. Barnes, M. Fielding, A.A. Hill, B. Haycocks, E. Bennet, Mr Mason, A. Harrap. Front row: S.H. Hyde, S.A. Oldham, N. Lewellyn, J. Higginbottom, A. Beard, J. Harrison, R. Cooper, B. Garnett.

An accident at Millbrook Bridge, Tintwistle in the 1930s. The vehicle, which was owned by H. Mitchell of Thurgoland had a speed restriction of 16 mph. Perhaps Harry Hancock from the village is asking the driver how it was possible to have an accident at that speed!

Another accident at Millbrook Bridge. Perhaps the steep incline from the village was too much for the brakes of this vehicle.

The fire at Bridge Mill in 1899. The mill was a major employer and the fire was a tragedy for the village.

Bridge Mill, Tintwistle in 1880. During the First World War the building on the left was used as a guncotton factory.

Four

People

Mrs Brown of Broadbottom Hall in 1980 celebrated the 300th anniversary of the building of the Hall by planting beech trees in the grounds with the assistance of her family and the author.

"I have seen death so often that it is not strange or painful to me. I am glad to die for my Country."

BRUSSELS, *October 12th,* 1915.

A printed silk card bearing the last words of Edith Cavell as a memorial to the men of the area who lost their lives in the First World War.

Mr and Mrs Bromley standing at the door of their cottage, 7 Church Brow, Mottram. Mr Bromley was the local postman for many years.

Spout Green, Mottram, against the bank of the small water lodge which fed the 'Spout', on the right. Members of the Broady family are on the left and those of the Mettricks on the right. The young woman on the right, in the white blouse, is 'Ewie' Berry's mother, Mary Hinchcliffe.

Ada Lawson of Broadbottom, like many women during the First World War, took on a job previously held by a man, that of postal deliveries. Sadly she died, at twenty-six, in 1918.

'Ewie' Berry and Kathleen Hartle in front of the White House in Spout Green.

Broadbottom men collecting coal at a dredge mine during the 1926 miners' strike. Derbyshire's 50,000 miners were paid strike money at the rate of 15/- per man, 7/6 per youth, 2/- for children under 14 years. Union funds of £250,000 were used up in four weeks.

The rear of Mottram Hall in 1907. David Hall, the agent for the estate, is third from the left on the back row. The estate comprised both Mottram and Thorncliffe Halls and was owned by Sir Samuel Hill Wood of Glossop.

'Ewie' Berry's father, Mr W.E.G. Berry.

Charles Ervin Booth and his wife Emily (*née* Nuttall) lived at High View, War Hill, Mottram. Charles Booth, largely self-educated after the age of eleven, worked as a railwayman at Hadfield Station. One of his tasks was to walk from Hadfield Station to Crowden where he hung lights on the level crossing – a long walk! He was an early socialist, a member of the I.L.P. and a radical poet (one of his poems is printed on page 6). Emily was the daughter of John Nuttall, sexton of Mottram Church in the 1880s. She built High View herself largely with money she earned as a 'wet nurse' to local wealthy families. The daughters of the family were weavers at Broad Mills, Broadbottom and the sons worked as clerks in the Lancashire and Yorkshire Railway. Emily's sister, Margaret Ann, was the last landlady of the Black Bull, against the church wall, Mottram which was eventually closed down by the autocratic Canon Miller.

Arthur Hague and family of Wimberry Hill Farm, Glossop.

A cottage near to the Picturedrome, Hadfield in the 1920s. In the picture, from left to right, are: -?-, 'Ewie' Berry, Tom Bennett, Sam Bennett, Mrs Berry, Jane Elliott.

Dancing troupe, Mottram village. Emma Swann was the troupe organiser. Back row, left to right: Doris Wilson, Joyce Redfern, Doris Keating, Emma Swann, Elsie Reeves, Glenda Bromley, Joe Swann. Middle row: Ivy Whittaker, Joan Walker, Betty Marsden, Margaret Bentley. Front row: Eric Peel, Irene Townley, Ronald Duckworth, Joe Keating, Joe Batty.

New York Cottages, Long Lane, Charlesworth in the 1920s. The site is now a car park for the Catholic Church, just before Besthill Bridge. Mrs Lee is seen with her daughter Ella.

The Shepherds Meeting, Millers Arms, Saltersbrook, Longdendale in 1907. Farmers from the surrounding areas met at this spot between Longdendale and Upper Derwent Valley to exchange stray sheep.

A sign of the Depression, 1920s.

The Commercial Inn, Crowden, with a group ready for the outing.

Mr and Mrs Miller, reservoir keeper, Longdendale.

Herman Fox and family, Ash Tree Farm, Crowden.

Crowden Hall. From left to right: Mr Turner, Mr Metcalf, Mr Wood.

Eddie and Annie Bagshaw, proprietors of the George and Dragon, Woodhead.

Len Ford, Tintwistle 1915.

Funeral of Tom Sidebottom, of Etherow House, Hollingworth, passing Arnfield Reservoir, Tintwistle in 1908.

Alf Wilson, 1st Winner, Nichols Cup 1910, Tintwistle.

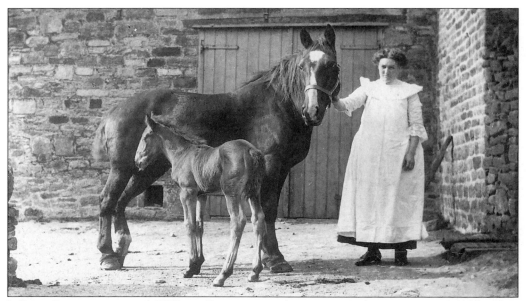

Lillian Garnett, sister of William Barnett, gamekeeper at Ogden House, Arnfield Moor, Tintwistle.

Jim Stafford and Lizzie, North Britain Farm in the late 1920s.

Mrs Shepley and Jim Chatterton on Woolley Mill Lane in the late 1920s.

Walter Hague, son of James Hague, and his family Higher Bank Farm.

Walkers in the Higher Bank Farm, Tintwistle area. This was a popular venue for locals with a break for tea at one of the farms. The three farms in the area were Higher, Lower and Middle Bank, all were later demolished by Manchester Corporation.

Ernest Hague, Higher Bank Farm.

Raymond Hartle, Lower Bank Farm, early 1920s.

James Hague, Higher Bank Farm.

The Revd W. Pemberton and his wife, a very popular Vicar of Mottram in the early 1900s. The Vicarage was then at the bottom of Church Brow opposite the school house, it was a fine building with a carriage drive, stables and rose garden. All that is there now to remind us of the past is its front wall and stone gate posts. A terrace of four cottages and two end cottages now cover the site, these were built by John Jackson, previously landlord of the Pack Horse Inn, then owner of Warhill Farm. His son Joe Jackson lived in the terrace for many years.

The hounds at Hillend House. Left to right: Mr Lowe (huntsman), J.W. Cowley (whipper in) Mr Harold Chapman (Gent), Mr and Mrs Jack Chapman (Gent) from Carlecotes, George Wood. John Chapman, their grandfather, died in 1877. In 1836 he married his cousin Annie Sidebottom, daughter of George Sidebottom of Hillend House. He was the largest shareholder of the Sheffield and Lincolnshire Railway Co., and financially supported the company in difficult times during the cutting of the Woodhead Tunnel. Amongst other estates he purchased Carlecotes in 1847. An extremely benevolent man, he introduced many schemes to assist the local community.

The staff of Mrs Greenwood's Cafe, Market Street, Mottram. Back row, left to right: Lilly Malpas, Ivy Radcliffe, Jenny Dawson. Front: Clara Whittaker, Margaret Cowley, Mrs Greenwood.

Frank Roberts, Longdendale Reservoir keeper.

Dan Lund, Arnfield Farm, 1890-1900.

Filling the water cart from the trough on Woodhead Road. Jim Cooper is on the left.

Thomas Edwin Winterbottom, born in
New Road, Tintwistle, 16 June 1893.

Ronald and Norman Chadwick of Woodhead Road, Tintwistle.

Mrs James Hague, aged 80, Higher Bank Farm, 4 March 1930.

The BBC radio *Gardeners Question Time* team in the garden of Etherow Lodge, Hollingworth. From left to right: Clay Jones, 'Trish' (Ken Ford's secretary), Stephan Buczacki, Bill Sowerbutts and Ken Ford (producer).

Bill Sowerbutts in his greenhouse at Etherow Lodge. Bill was born on Ashton Moss in a house bought by his father in 1892. Being so involved from an early age in the family business of breeding poultry, growing celery and other vegetables and flowers, and also marketing them, gave him the wide experience that he later drew on in his broadcasts and books. Bill started his gardening broadcasts in 1947.

Frank Thornhill and son at Throstle Nest, Hollingworth in the 1950s.

Mrs Ellison of Rose Bank, Hollingworth.

Love from Hadfield

How we are longing for the day
When we shall see you here;
With those who dearly love you,
Who in thought with you are ne...

Tree planting ceremony outside the Medical Centre, 1973, Hollingworth, undertaken by Silvester Ellison, penultimate Chairman of Longdendale UDC and actress Pat Phoenix, who was resident on Wedneshough Green for many years. She appeared in fashionable, and perhaps rather theatrical, style, wearing a suede coat with fur trimmings, flared trousers and white boots.

A postcard from a loved one in Hadfield during the First World War.

Five

Leisure

An exhibition in June 1977 organised by Mottram villagers to honour L.S. Lowry RA who died in 1976 after living in the village for twenty-eight years.

Mottram Show officials.

Church Brow, Mottram in the 1950s. People assemble outside the old schoolhouse for Mottram church sermons.

Hollingworth carnival, 1900s. Mrs Jackson is wearing the striped shawl and they are all standing on Mottram Moor.

Golf pavilion, The Hague, Broadbottom in the 1920s, is now converted to a dwelling.

Brookfield Sunday School AFC, 1900s. Back row, left to right: F. Sellars (secretary), R. Sheppard, R. Stockdale, G. Clarke, H. Clayton, J. Shepperd, H. Sellars (committee), H. Coxon, M. Darwent (linesman).

Crowden AFC, 1913-14. Some names are remembered: back row, left to right: No.3 Joe Wood, No.4 George Bamford, No.5 Arthur Wood (goalkeeper). Front row: No.1 G.J. Brocklehurst, No.4 Harry Hambleton, No.6 Walter Brocklehurst, No.8 Johnny Dodson.

Shooting cabin, Black Clough, Woodhead.

A gathering of men at the
Ashopton Inn.

The George and Dragon Inn, Woodhead seen here in 1960 and now demolished. Left to right: Barbara Hancock's husband, Eddie Tunnicliffe, Barbara Hancock, -?-, Mrs Bagshaw (landlady), -?-.

George and Dragon Inn, 1960. Left to right: Ann Bainbridge, -?-, Barbara Cooper, Lilly Nicholls, Mrs Bagshaw, -?-.

Tintwistle Harriers pose in a mock 'start'.

Tintwistle Harriers in the late 1920s. Jim Byron of Millbrook House is presenting the Cup to Jim Thompson.

Tintwistle Church League champions, 1911.

The Cheshire Regiment, 1913 with some Tintwistle men; in the back row: J. Pogson, (centre with moustache), Sgt Major H. Brand. Front left: J. Bagshaw.

Holiday Camp, near Townhead Farm, Tintwistle.

Tintwistle Independent Church team, 1933-34.

Tintwistle Cricket Club, 1920s.

A crowd awaiting the carnival parade in Manchester Road, Tintwistle, 1904.

The St John's Ambulance float, Tintwistle Carnival, 1949.

Before the match was struck at Tintwistle celebrations for Edward VII's Jubilee.

The band leads a Sunday School procession in Market Street, Hollingworth.

Tintwistle band at Millbrook House. The tall man in the back row is Jack Haythorn, gardener at the house.

Hollingworth AFC, 1927-28. Back row, left to right: H. Thomason (trainer), ? Ibbotson, Arthur Hartley, S. Dewsnap, Edwin Ball, Tommy Makin, Ernest Ollerenshaw (manager), H. Lambert (secretary). Front row: ? Lever (reserve), Maurice Moran, Teddy Bennett, Jack Hill, Pat Bennett, Willy Broadhurst, J. Wood.

Woolley Bridge Mission AFC, 1911-12.

'Ye Old Farm Yard', Hollingworth Carnival float.

Outside Mr Sidebottom's Etherow House on Carnival Day in Hollingworth.

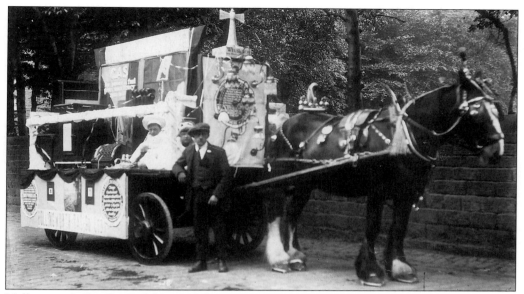

Hollingworth Gas Co. Ltd Carnival float.

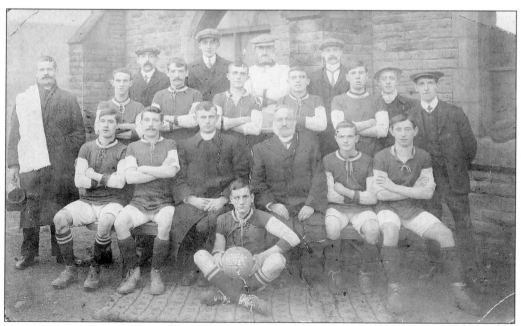

Hollingworth St Mary's AFC, 1902.

Hollingworth Liberal Club Whist team, 1905.

Hollingworth Cricket Club, early 1900s.

Hollingworth men on an outing driven by W. Merrill in his waggonette. The cottages in the background were on the site of the present car park for the New Inn, an area known previously as 'The Knowl'.

Spring Street Methodist Chapel Sunday School, Hollingworth, late 1800s.

St Mary's Hollingworth, Sunday School Parade turning into Wedneshough Green, late 1800s.

Hollingworth Carnival floats outside the Manor House in the 1920s.

Dinting Church of England schoolboys cricket team, 3 July 1922. Back row, left to right: E. Sidebottom, H. Isaacs, N. Hibbert, T. Thornley. Middle row: S. Yeomans, S. Goddard, W. Chorlton, H. Barnes, E. Humphries. Front row: S. Bamforth, M. Bickerdyke, H. Hobson, J. Platt, H. Gilson.

Charlesworth Church of England hockey team when the school still taught all ages.

Glossop Youth Club at Whitfield in the late 1940s. Firth Bamforth, the Youth Leader, is in the centre.

Six

Institutions

Some of the 400 children who planted 10,000 trees on seven acres of land in one day in 1978 to commemorate the Queen's Jubilee.

Mottram church bellringers in the 1900s. They maintained a proud record of teams, in the 1800s, for the number of changes made in the peals.

The unveiling of Broadbottom War Memorial, Moss Lane on 1 July 1922. Note the absence of poppy wreaths. The British Legion had not yet introduced these commemorative tokens.

Mottram church bells 1910. They were renovated and rehung by Taylor & Co. of Loughborough.

The completed memorial, with stone carving atop, is now in place. The iron railings were removed in the Second World War, supposedly, to be melted down for the war effort.

Broadbottom School, 1937. An informal photograph with, back row, left at rear: -?-, Ronnie Hackney, Joyce Maw, Harry Barnett (shading eyes), Clifford Yarwood, Donald Wright, Ronnie Kershaw, Arthur Thornley, Leslie Maw, Dennis Jones, Eric Sidebottom. Middle row: Derek Parkey, Margaret Smith, Shelia Braddock, Eric Wroe, Mona Braddock, Derek Braddock behind, Jackie Rogers, Fred Smith, Vera Capper, Jack Lemmon. Front row: Rhona Marden, Margaret Rhodes, Vera Stafford.

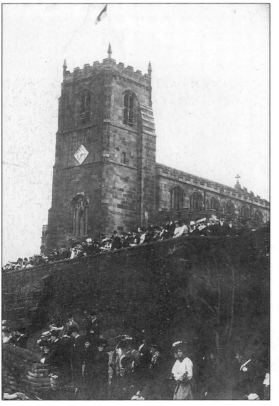

Mottram church sermons, 1900s.

116

Members of the Glossop and District Christian Endeavour Union, 1924.

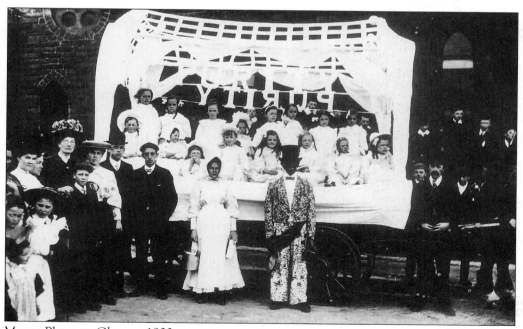

Mount Pleasant, Glossop, 1900.

Padfield School, 1900s.

Padfield School, 1900s.

Crowden School, 1914. Unfortunately a mouse chewed the original list of children in the photograph! The teachers were Miss Clarke on the left and Mrs Wood on the right.

St Johns Church of England school, Charlesworth, 1947. Back row, left to right: Mrs D. Clark (Headmistress), Sydney Barnes, Peter Brown, Derek Newton, Bob Porter, Mrs A. Dewsnap (Infant teacher). Third row: Ena Porter, Jean Salt, Joy Price, Peggy Rowbottom, Sylvia Seckington, Pearl Tetlow. Second row: Malcolm Porter, Sheila Broadbent, Elizabeth Higginbottom, Pamela Beard, Brenda Cochrane, Roy Porter, Tony Bamforth. Front row: Tom Shaw, Charles Price, Tojo (the dog), Ronnie ?, Albert Fenton. It's not possible to comment on the habits of the children in the photograph but it is remembered that Tojo used to chew the childrens' socks!

Crowden School, 1916. The list (saved by the mousetrap), back row, left to right: Ed Booth, -?-, Maggie Darwin, -?-, Lessie Wood, Renie Darwin, Bill Brocklehurst, Harold Carver. Second row: Mrs Wood, Miss Darwin, Bill Wood, Sara Gee, Hilda Fisher, Annie Wood, Jim Gee, Jack Rhodes, Hilda Rhodes, Miss Wain. Front row: -?-, -?-, Ben Sykes, Win Davies, John Davies, Phil Beaver, Billy Shaw, Laurie Dodson, Mary Shaw, Tom Gee, Nora Dodson.

St Johns Church of England school, Charlesworth, 1959. Back row, left to right: Lee Thompson, Valerie Newsham, Sandra Caine, Joan Fairest, Geraldine Davies, Barbara Morris, Stuart Robertson (?), Mrs Dewsnap (Teacher). Middle row: Martyn Brocklehurst, Ronnie Deary, -?-, Peter Bee, Keith McIlroy, Clive Hallam, Miles Robinson, George Newsham, David Smith. Front row: Teresa Newsham, Ruth Morris, Vivienne Hepworth, Janet Williams, Hilary Thompson, Lynda Caine, Louise Davies. What a happy looking group of children!

Woodhead church, pre-1924. The church was founded in 1487 by Sir Edmund Shaw who, on moving to London, made a fortune and became Lord Mayor and Jeweller to Edward IV. Over the years the fabric of the building has suffered, and been repaired many times. It is in a poor state once more, the extremes of the elements being mainly to blame. Many of the navvies who were killed while cutting the Woodhead Tunnels are buried here.

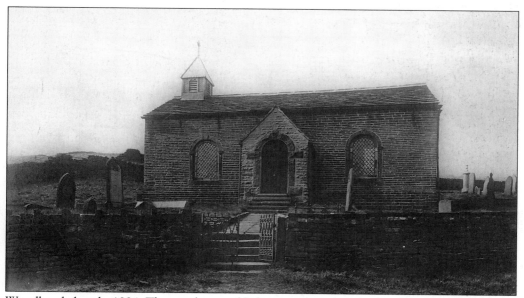

Woodhead church, 1924. The porch was added as a memorial to the local men who died in the First World War.

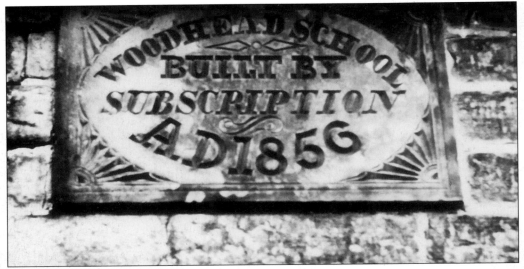

Date stone of Woodhead School.

Tintwistle Scouts, 1920s. W. Swallow was the scoutmaster.

Tintwistle Independent School, 1957. Back row, left to right: A. Dyler, L. Bowers, S. Bennett, E. Cockayne, H. Greatorix, D. Harrop, N. Price, J. Chatterton, S. James, Mrs Tongue. Second row: M. Harrop, A. Bennett, R. Edge, B. Rowbottom, C. Newman, A. Newman, Mr Evans. Third row: D. Bowers, H. Chatterton, B. Bennett, F. Cockayne, S. James, M. Smith, L. Brierley. Front row: N. Booth, -?-, -?-, R. Cockayne.

Village fire engine, Tintwistle, 1930.

Tintwistle Church School infants, 1932.

The British School, Tintwistle.

The Independent School, Old Road, Tintwistle.

Tintwistle Church School, 1920s.

Tintwistle Church School, 1928.

War Memorial, Tintwistle. Note the conductor's position on a wheelbarrow.

Hollingworth chapel and manse.

St Mary's, Hollingworth, Church Girls' Brigade, 1932.

The Girls' Friendly Society, Tintwistle Church Sunday School, 1925. The photograph was taken as a memento for Mrs Fairhurst who was leaving the church, following the death of her husband, the vicar. Back row, left to right (married names in brackets): ? Hinchcliffe, Doris Ralph, Marion Hinchcliffe, ? Hodgson (Mrs Sharp), Clara Platt (Mrs Hollingworth), ? Crowton, Ada Brocklehurst (Mrs Hancock). Middle row: ? Willis, Ann Snape, Jane Lee, Mrs Fairhurst (vicar's wife), Bessie Sharp (Mrs Wildgoose), Lily Brocklehurst (Mrs Nicholls), Emma Miller (Mrs Salthouse). Front row: Annie Brocklehurst (Mrs Bagshaw of the George and Dragon), Dora Hampshire, Emily Woodcock (Mrs Smith), Alice Haig (Mrs Ralph), Emma Sharp, Alice Nicholls (Mrs Thornhill), Lillian Warhurst (Mrs Walker), Emma Lee, May Nicholls (Mrs Bennett), Ena Carson, ? Lee.